S

I want to thank everyone who worked so selflessly; putting your own time and energy into making the book Transcended become a reality. Thank you for your labor of love and for putting up with a hard headed guy like me. My heartfelt thanks goes to:

- Brent
- Kathy
- Dale
- Leland
- Debbie
- Pat
- Bob

As well as the many others who gave input and were influential.

Most of all, I wish to express very special thanks for the love and support of Kim, who stood by me to see this dream and goal of mine become a living reality. And to God, for without Him, this experience would not have happened in the first place!

God Bless

Vern Gray

2016

Vernon Gray
ark0924@gmail.com

1

I wrote this book because I wanted to reach out and let everyone know about my experience when God reached out to me. I did not write this book for the church; this really has nothing to do with the church or about the church. It is simply to let everyone know about the reality of heaven; that it is a very real place, not just imaginary. People actually live there after they leave this earth, and I found out firsthand about how real God is.

Like me, you may be wondering why I was chosen to go. All I can say is what God said to me: "I have brought you here so you can go back and tell everyone on earth that I am real and so is heaven." So, enjoy reading *Transcended*!

I lay on the floor thinking about what had just happened to me. How would I be able to explain it? I was puzzled but I knew it *had* happened. I knew God had taken me to heaven.

As I thought about writing this book and how I might explain it, I was not sure how I would introduce my experience in heaven where God lives. Many people have their own ideas about heaven. They may have seen it portrayed in a movie or read about it in a book. In fact, there are many books written about heaven and a number of movies also.

I know of a place called heaven because I have experienced it. It is far beyond the starry skies. One summer years ago, a friend and I were lying on the grass looking up at the stars. She said, "*I wonder what's up there?*" Then jokingly, I looked at her and said, "*That's where the starship Enterprise is, dummy, don't you know that?*" Through our laughter, we kept looking up and smiling. I then grew very serious and said, "*No, that is where heaven is! That is also where God lives.*" At this point I was only going by what other people would say; I was really just showing off.

Some people imagine God sitting on His throne giving orders. They may think that He will throw lightning bolts and zap them into the abyss if they were bad. You need to know that God is not like that.

To others, heaven is a place of tranquility and peace. You may have your own picture of heaven in your mind what you think it should be. Now let me describe to you *my* experience; of how I was **transcended** into heaven.

Does it really exist? Can I go?

People everywhere want to go to heaven when they hear about it. You can just mention the word *heaven*, and it brings new meaning to the notion of life after death. Could there be a place beyond our wildest imaginations and our dreams? Is there more to our life than what we know down here? Some movies imply that both good *and* bad people can go to heaven. Is this true? Well since heaven is God's house, I'm certain He has his own standards for who will go heaven, not man.

Some ask *is there really a heaven?* Others wonder *is heaven only a state of our mind, or is it possible it even exists?* I say heaven *does* exist, and it is a wonderful and real place! You may be thinking, *well, how does he know all about this*? I know because I have experienced heaven firsthand, and it is a real place, full of unbelievable sights and sounds. There is not a care in the world when you are there. If you think this is too good to be true or that I have made it all up in my head, I hope you will think again and hear what I have to tell and show you.

Reflect with me on what happens at a funeral. There is a lot of sadness in our hearts when someone dies. The family is grieving. Some of us do not know what to say so we sit quietly and wait. People express their grief in many different ways. Some people cry uncontrollably, throwing themselves on the casket, refusing to let go. Grief is a natural process that people go through. Most of the time grief will accompany the loss of someone dear.

It is hard to grasp that we will never see that person again. However, it is a fact that we will all die! We will find ourselves at the end of our own lives on that appointed day. That date we have with death cannot ever be stopped. No one can avoid taking that last breath on earth. We all will have to let go of someone through death, and even let go of ourselves when it is our time to go from this earth.

Death is an eternal reality that separates us from life as we know it here on earth. No one knows when his or hers last breath on earth will be. It just happens! You could be riding on a bus or a train, driving a car, even flying in an airplane or walking in a mall.

If we knew our exact time of death, we might have a different outlook on life. We might show one another more kindness and love and appreciate our families. Maybe some of us would write journals to leave for our loved ones or close friends. We could fill them up with stories of special memories of our lives. I am sure if we knew when we would die, we would leave something behind for our loved ones. We might let them know just how much we appreciated them being in our lives. These things that should be cherished for generations to come, even by relatives who never really knew us personally or simply did not have time to get to know us.

One day we all may find ourselves faced with having to let go of someone dear. No longer will we see their smiles or faces. No longer will we hear their voices or laughter. We cannot visit them to share our experiences. They are gone forever!

Death leaves us with only memories of them, and time will cause memories to fade. Some of us hold on to the memory of loved ones by keeping their personal belongings and refusing to let go. These things may comfort us and bring fond memories, but then the reality of death sets in, and the recognition that someday we all must die. Death means gone forever from this life, to start a new life.

I think knowing this truth is what makes heaven so appealing. There is hope that springs forth in us when we hear that we can one day be reunited with loved ones who have passed away. It is comforting to say the least. Deep in the corners of your mind you may be asking yourself *where did they go and where are they now?* Then it gets personal, and you turn your thoughts inward and start to wonder, *where will I go when it is* my *time to die?*

If any of us knew when death was going to come knocking on our door, who knows, we might do some of the fun things we had only dreamed about; such as traveling to other countries, spending more time with family and friends, or even seeing distant relatives.

Most of us do not want to talk about death. We are not ready to encounter it. We just go on living as if tomorrow will always be there. Some of us do not even bother to write out a will so that our wishes would be carried out!

I will ask you to stop for a moment right now and think about your last day on this earth. What will happen to you when you die? How will your family handle you being gone? Will you leave behind memories to warm their hearts and comfort them? Or will you leave behind nothing? Are you prepared for your date with death?

These questions should cause you to be curious about my experience in heaven. I know what heaven is like because I went there. I will share with you some of the things I experienced while in that place called heaven.

Many movies portray heaven as a place of eternal bliss. Furthermore, they show that we can all go there after death. I cannot judge anybody, for *I am not God*! However, I can tell you about my own experience in heaven.

This is my story, and it is true. I went to heaven! I would like to explain how I went and what happened to me. I had an *out of body* experience. You may be skeptical. However, I will ask you before you shut your mind to the possibility of such an experience—or even life after death in a place called heaven—to read my story.

My experience of going to heaven changed my life forever. I am not the same man, meaning it was very encouraging to know where I will be going when I die. I will never fear dying as long as there is breath in me. After visiting heaven, I eagerly anticipate going back when my life on earth is over. I have seen and now know what awaits me when I die.

So, sit back and relax as I take you there with me, through these pages. Heaven seems so far away, but in reality, it is just a breath away. I will take you on my journey of a lifetime and have you wondering about life after death!

TABLE OF CONTENTS

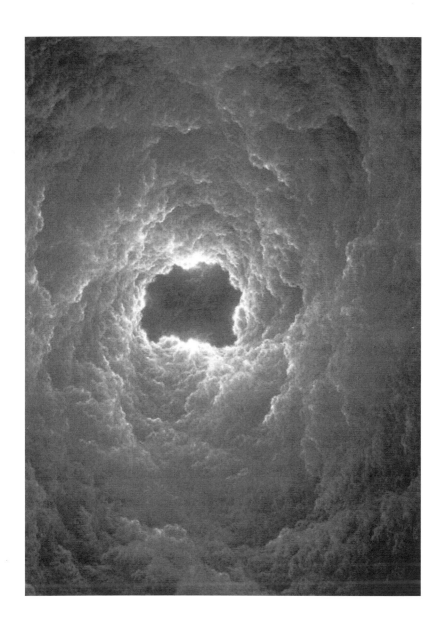

EXPERIENCE 1 - THE ENTRANCE

The experience that forever changed my life began in Dallas, Texas, on a hot summer day. Anyone who has been there knows about that heat. There were normal activities going on that day. People were outside talking, walking, and laughing. There were planes flying high above the city. *This is just an ordinary day*, I thought. Nevertheless, this day would end up like no other day. I would never have dreamt that my day, and my life, were about to change forever.

I was in my study preparing for an upcoming meeting. As I continued studying, the stage was set. There I was, lying on the floor studying with my notebook, pens, highlighters and Bible opened. The only other living thing in that room besides me was Samson, my Russian Blue cat. He was stretched out lying next to me chewing on my notebook. Samson's personality was such that he walked around as if he owned the place. In fact, he did. I can honestly say that Samson was one of a kind. I never had another pet like him.

As I continued studying, a presence came into the room that made the atmosphere change. I knew that something was different. It made me feel relaxed, like someone without a care in the world. The air was thick and there was such energy and strength that came upon me; even through me. It was something I had never experienced before. I was wide-awake, and I wondered, *what is this I am feeling*? This presence caused all the pressure and stress to leave my body and I felt total peace. It was amazing how relaxed I felt, to say the least. A peace came over me that no words can describe. I felt very free in my body and mind – free as a bird.

You may be asking, *what was that presence?* (More about that later) Or, you may be wondering, *why was he picked to experience this?* Wherever you are in life, you can come to know the reality of heaven; that it is a real place. Some of the questions you might have about heaven will likely be answered upon reading my book. I challenge you to have an open mind about my experience.

Now, let us get back to my experience and what I felt and how it affected me. This presence changed the atmosphere in the room. There was new life and energy that came alive within me and on me. It overwhelmed every fiber of my being! I felt that I was being subdued totally. I felt assurance and strength. There was total peace within my mind. It seemed as if I knew where I was, but I was somewhere else. My mind was very alert and clear.

On this day, that presence changed my life forever. **The room seemed to be filled with a thick cloud, and it was enveloping me.** This presence grew stronger and stronger and I knew without any doubt that this was a visitation from the Almighty God. It was unlike anything I had ever experienced. The presence grew still stronger yet and overtook me, causing my body to change. It caused me to start to leave my physical body. Now I was being lifted up by that power. My spirit went right up. I felt free, without any limitations, free like the clouds, or a bird flying through the air. I felt light!

As I began to travel upward, I could see everything below. I could see my physical body lying by my cat Samson, who looked as if he had been knocked out cold. At first, it appeared that I was about eight feet above my body. I started to climb higher, sailing right through the ceiling and roof, onward to the outside of the building. Just imagine, I sailed right through all those things in the ceilings and was not affected in the least. Once outside, I felt the heat and could hear the noises of the city, along with the birds chirping, horns honking and people talking below me.

You may be wondering, *how did I know it was hot?* And *how did I hear these sounds since I was no longer in my physical body?* When my spirit was out of my body, I felt intensely alive and my senses were heightened. I even saw that there were emergency vehicles traveling across the town. I could see children playing in the schoolyard down the street where I lived because I drove by there so many times that I recognized it instantly when I saw it. You could even see the playground from the street.

Right then my speed accelerated. I was traveling high above the earth and very fast. I saw a Southwest Airlines jet to the left of me, and I could even see the people through the windows. It was coming in to land at Love Field, making its final approach. As the jet was going down, I was going up—very fast, though I cannot estimate the speed. I kept going faster and faster. I felt something powerful pulling me upward. There are no words to describe it—I was flying through the air, without an airplane!

Imagine flying without wings. At one point, I began to feel even lighter, as if some sort of weight, like a body suit, had come off me. Let me explain. Perhaps you have felt the weight of a wet, heavy coat on you and you know that feeling of being weighed down like that. Well that is how I felt. Nevertheless, once it came off I felt even lighter and traveled even faster. I felt it through my whole being. I was feeling weightless in midair! Wow! What a feeling!

After that feeling of being weightless, I seemed to be inside an encasement of some sort with clouds all around me. I still had no fear of what was happening to me. I seemed to be going super-fast now. Then a tunnel appeared in my vision. Clouds were forming around me that grew thicker and thicker. I saw extremely bright lights; lights of blue, purple and gold inside them. They were the brightest lights I had ever seen. This presence of energy never left me while I went through the tunnel, but it was getting even stronger.

I never felt any fear while flying through this tunnel of clouds, this chamber—only perfect peace and energy. As I sped through it the lights grew brighter and brighter. It was not a blinding brightness; it was pleasant to my eyes. I could still hear, see, and feel everything that was happening as I experienced pure energy.

Then in one blink of an eye, I was at the end of the tunnel. For some reason I thought I was being taken to heaven. Never having seen anything like this in my life, I still knew this was the entrance to some place. Before me appeared a person who resembled a man. He seemed about eight feet tall and three feet wide to me. He was not your average person! Somehow, I knew he was an angel. I also knew I was with him in heaven! Standing next to him as big and bright, I never had any feeling of fear of him, but I could see this angel had some type of authority. There was a glow around him. His skin was the color of bronze, and he had long golden-blonde hair. I even touched his hair and told him how I liked it. He looked at me in a strange way. There was no doubt that he was definitely all male. No thoughts were on my mind about my home or the earth I had left. None of that mattered to me at all.

Now doesn't that sound strange? Here my spirit was in heaven while my body was back in my study on the floor in Texas—and I did not care. It was reminiscent of the song, "Fly Me To The Moon"—the only thing was, I had been flown to Heaven! Man has been to the moon and there is nothing there for us. People have been to heaven and come back and say there is everything for us! It's like this; you go to the MOON! As for me, I'm going to HEAVEN!

At this point I never wanted to go back to earth. It was furthest thing from my mind. Who in their right mind would want to go back to earth after visiting heaven? I said "Heaven, what heaven? Are you kidding?" I felt overwhelmed and overjoyed. Being caught up into this place made me feel young again and full of energy.

Somehow, this angel knew my name, which amazed me. The angel said, "Vernon, God has called you up here today concerning the questions you have been asking him about the Bible, heaven, and the healing gift you have—questions like *who, what, where, when* and *why*."

I said "*What*! *Are you kidding me*? I said, *God. What do you mean*?"

The angel then told me, "You will experience what heaven is like so you will be able to tell people all over the world about it and, (even though they will call you nuts,) that this place is what God has designed for all mankind." After his words, I knew that this was just a visit, and I would not be staying here very long. I knew I would be going back home.

Questions were beginning to enter my mind. I wanted to know everything. It seemed so unreal, but the questions I had were being answered *as I thought them*. I will explain this to you, as we get further into my experience. There were so many things I wanted to know and like most people, I can be very inquisitive!

The angel said, "You will now know, see, and hear many things. Each one will be explained to you, as well as how it relates to the people on earth."

Now you may be sitting on the edge of your seat thinking, *is this person for real? Are there really angels out there*? However, there was one standing right in front of me, minus his wings. I have seen angels at certain times in my life. I do not know why I have been someone chosen to see these spiritual beings called heaven's angels, but I am glad I am!

Now I know that heaven is a real place, full of unbelievable things. In my natural mind, it was hard to understand what I was seeing. Some people may have their own ideas of what heaven should be like. Personally, I've always believed in heaven because of what I had read in the Bible. Now here I am being chosen to go there and experience it firsthand proved what I have believed. Heaven is not like the image most people have of it. Some think there are angels flying through the air singing fa-la-la-la, or sitting on clouds and playing harps.

Heaven is not like that! It is a real city where people actually live and enjoy life. The major difference that I observed in heaven is that nothing dies. Also, no one ever seems sad and they are not homesick for earth as if you and I would be when we take a long trip away from our natural home.

You know how when you are gone, you start to miss your bed? Your surroundings are different and you miss your favorite chair in front of the T.V. If you have a pet that lays in your lap, well he will miss you too. It's home and there is a great saying, "there is no place like home". That's exactly the way it is in heaven. Everyone that you see in heaven is happy, they have peace and are full of life, as though heaven is their home and it is where they belong.

Angels are my real heroes. I would like to share a real life experience that happened to me that demonstrates just how powerful they are, whether you see them or not.

It was a Wednesday evening and I was driving to church. My wife and I were on the freeway, I 35 North I as I recall. We were traveling down the road in the left lane, the fast lane. The weather was nice, the road was dry and all was good. All of a sudden, from the other side of the freeway, a car hit the side of the wall, flew up into the air and flipped upside down. It was just inches from landing on top of our car. We had a birds eye view of the guy and girl in the other car. We were looking at each other through the windshield and you could just see the terror on their faces. There was no time to do anything now. But then, all of a sudden, the car raised up and flew back over the fence and landed on all four wheels.

Now I was in a trance-like state and still driving. I have always wondered why I didn't stop the car. All I can remember saying out loud to my wife is; *"I am cut, I am cut."* It felt like my arms were all cut up. She said, *"pull off at the next exit and let's check and see."* Then she said, *"what just happened?"* I got out and looked at the car. There were no dents or scratches, no broken glass, and my arms were not bleeding. I was thinking, *how could this be?* We got back in the car and went on to church.

Now the service had already begun and we went in and sat down behind a lady. We were still in a daze to say the least. The pastor said, *"lets all thank the Lord for watching over us."* I said out loud, *"You have no idea what we just went thru!"* Then all of a sudden, the lady in front of us, jumped up and turned towards us, smiled real big and said, *"when you two sat down I heard God say to me I sent my angels to save them tonight, you tell them."*

Luke 4:10 (MSG)

'He has placed you in the care of angels to protect you;

And so she did. I sat there in total amazement the rest of the service holding my wife's hand. Right after the services we told that lady the whole story about our experience. Needless to say, she was amazed when she heard it. She thanked God for sending His angels to our rescue.

Now, the next story I would like to share with you concerns one of the darkest days ever that America had to experience. You may have heard other stories of how God sent his angels to save people.

The date was September 11, 2001. The location was the World Trade Center in New York City. As I stood there three weeks later, in the midst of the destruction, it looked like a war zone. Sadness hung over the city like a cloak. I thought about the loss of life, and the hundreds yet unaccounted for. The thought shocked me, and I became aware of how valuable life is.

How horrible that day must have been for those who were there, not knowing whom to trust, where to go, or who to turn to. Many people wandered around aimlessly like zombies. I also saw their fear of the unknown and their future. The expressions on their faces showed me they did not know what might happen next. It was such a hopeless situation for America, in my opinion.

As I stood there weeks after those terrible events, questions arose in my mind. I asked God through my own tears and heartache, *"Why, God, why?"* I waited eagerly for his reply. I sensed his peace as he talked to me. He said, *"When Jesus came into the world that's when peace came, son, but there are evil men in this world who train themselves to destroy people and things. It was the evil within their hearts that flew those planes into those towers."*

Ecclesiastes 9:12 (MSG)

No one can predict misfortune. Like fish caught in a cruel net or birds in a trap, so men and women are caught by accidents evil and sudden.

After the attack, I saw a story on the news about a man caught in one of the towers. He testified that when the second tower started to tumble down he saw a bright light. He followed this light to an opening. In all that devastation and darkness, can you imagine seeing a light? He said that he climbed through the wreckage toward the light, and it led him out to safety. The man exclaimed, "*It must have been an angel leading me out!*" He said he is alive because of that light. I agree with him "it must have been an angel." I am convinced that angels are here for us and that they carry out the plans of God. They are his agents, or I might say, his hands, extended to the earth. Even Mary, the mother of Jesus, had encountered an angel, who came and talked to her face-to-face.

Luke 2:10 (MSG)

Suddenly, God's angel stood among them and God's glory blazed around them. They were terrified. The angel said, "Don't be afraid. I'm here to announce a great and joyful event that is meant for everybody, worldwide: A Savior has just been born in David's town, a Savior who is Messiah and Master.

What did you think when those planes crashed through the World Trade Towers and when you saw the footage of the devastation live on TV? Did you think God did not care about us? Did you think more was going to happen in America? When any of us come to a place where we know circumstances are beyond our control, this is a good time to come to God and give Him a chance.

I know that I felt as if I were on a roller coaster ride, sitting on the edge of my seat—at first, climbing very slowly to the top, and then heading down extremely fast. That is how it is living in this world today. This is a good time to have an angel watching over us. We do not need to act as if we can do it on our own. Personally, I will take all the help I can get.

Now, let us get back to my experience in heaven. After passing through the tunnel of clouds and being at the entrance of heaven, I was standing there speechless, in awe of the angel before me. Then this angel began speaking to me. To my amazement, I understood him. I thought about what I had seen so far. To have this angel by my side communicating with me was awesome. He told me that he would be my escort. He said, *"You are to visit several places here."*

So he took my arm and guided me to a grassy area that led to a street. It was not like an ordinary street. It was bright, different from any street I had ever seen. It looked as if it were made of pure gold. Yes gold, think of the gold in the jewelry you wear. Now just imagine that you are walking on it. That is what I was experiencing. These streets looked as if thousands of lights them illuminated them from beneath

Revelation 21:21 (MSG)

The main street of the City was pure gold, translucent as glass.

The one I was on was transparent, and it looked as if you could fall right through it. These streets supported a whole city with both small and large buildings. There were beautiful trees and flowers. The colors were very vibrant and full of life. I could smell the sweet fragrance of heaven's flowers. I saw different types of flowers that appeared to be sitting in big wine barrels cut in half.

I saw children playing, and I heard them laugh. I seemed foreign to them, but they had no fear of me. Some even said hi and smiled at me. Children in heaven were happy. Never did I see any expressions of fear! Their faces radiated pure joy and excitement. It was as if nobody had a single care.

There was still so much more to see and experience. Every time I looked around, I saw something new and exciting.

I Corinthians 2:9 MSG

No one's ever seen or heard anything like this, never so much as imagined anything quite like it—What God has arranged for those who love him.

It was amazing! The angel got a strange look on his face whenever I said, *"Holy Cow! Look at that, will you?"* I can imagine him thinking, where did this person come from? And is he for real? As we continued to walk, I saw two men sitting on a bench carved inside of a tree. I got closer, and had to take a second look. *"Wow!"* I knew who these men were. I looked at the angel and said, *"That's Peter and John!"*

The Angel replied, *"Yes, and you know the Bible."* I was shocked that I had recognized them. I even said to myself, *"how did I know them"?* After all, this is the first time I have ever seen them! Sure, I read about them in the bible. As I stood wondering about all of this, the thought came to me that *the same Spirit that is in them is in me.* This is what I mean; when someone receives and believes in Jesus as God's Son, the Bible says that the spirit of Jesus comes inside their spirit to live. You see, I have done that, and that is why I knew who those men were. The same Spirit in them lives in me. I was so excited that all I wanted to do was ask more questions.

While I standing in front of Peter, a disciple of Jesus, all I could say was *"Tell me about Jesus!"* When I said that, his face lit up. It was as if a thousand lights were within him. He smiled broadly and said, *"Oh, you mean the Master of our souls."* I was so excited about what I heard from him about Jesus that I did not hear anything else he was saying.

It was utterly amazing, and no words can describe how caught up I was in at moment. You had to be there! For some reason, after that I felt as if my mind were shutting down. I thought about everything that was happening to me, and questioned myself: *Am I dreaming? Will I ever wake up? Is this really happening?*

I challenge you to find out more about heaven for yourself and seek your own experience; do not just take my word for it. My trip there was limited, but there is much more to tell. Also, keep in mind that there are some things I cannot disclose now, because they are not to be made known at this time. I will say this— God will in his own time-share them with the world. He might even show you.

Next, the angel took me to an entrance of a big wide place. This place made me feel all alone in a way I cannot explain. When I turned around, to my amazement the angel was gone! I was indeed alone in heaven for the first time. I said aloud, *"Where did he go?"* A dark and dreary feeling of silence and the loneliness I felt inside came upon me. The hall felt cold, and I felt like I was being pulled into it, as if it were something I had to go through. It felt like a tomb of some sort. The floor was made up of cobblestones of different shapes and sizes, put together like a puzzle. It was dark-red and seemed to have a green cast shadowing over it. There was not much light in the hall. *"This feels like the Judgment Hall!"* I said aloud.

As I walked through it, many events from my life came to mind—mostly bad things that I had said and done. I felt so much conviction and guilt! I was ashamed for the bad things I had done in my life. Even worse, they seemed magnified to me. I thought, *how could I have done or said such things.* This hall did not seem very long, but the experience could not end soon enough for me. I felt guilty, like an old dirty dog that needed a bath—inside as well outside. I think you get the picture.

After leaving the Judgment Hall, the next place was a room that I called the *records room*. Everything I had said or done on earth has all been recorded and my records were stored there. This room looked like a lawyer's room, with beautiful, dark, detailed wood. There were wood beams pressed together in arches, each decorated with gold ornaments, a Star of David and an oak leaf.

I noticed what appeared to be file cabinets lined up along the walls, and rows of cabinets were in the center of the room, they were all set in perfect rows. They appeared to be the color of bronze, and on each drawer, I saw a brass plate. This brass plate had an inscription of some sort in what looked to me like Hebrew lettering. I noticed that each one only had four letters stamp on the drawers. There were some lights in the room, then all of sudden an even brighter light appeared in that room.

That is when I heard a voice speaking with authority saying. *"Vernon, I brought you here today to answer some of the questions son, that you've been asking me."* As this voice was speaking, I began to hear another noise and some of the drawers began to open up. As I turned and looked at the drawers, there was a light shining from inside them. I knew this was the voice of God, for I had heard it before. I could not see God, but I knew he was there and his presence was what I felt, and that it was God himself speaking to me.

By now, you might be thinking, *Oh sure, it was God's voice!* In my case, a person would have to be spiritually blind, deaf, or just plain stupid not to know this was The Creator's voice. Now I am not calling anybody stupid, I just know His voice. He called me by my name. He spoke very clear english to me. I understood Him totally. If you have any doubt, Moses also heard the voice of God—and he understood it.

Deuteronomy 5:26 (MSG)

We've seen that God can speak to humans and they can still live.

Let me tell you something about his voice: It is different. It speaks with authority. When he spoke to me, he sounded like a judge, a father, and a friend all together. I knew I was standing in the presence of the Creator. This really caught my attention and I will never forget it. I can truly say my heart was touched.

God truly knows all about us. Then God said, "*All that you see here are records. Everything you have ever done or said is here and has all been recorded, since the beginning of your existence. For I have seen it all and I know it all. There is nothing hidden from me, nothing that I have not witnessed. All the activities of men and women who have tried to hide their deeds from me. Since the beginning of time, I have acknowledged all their lives. My eyes pierce the darkness and I can see through the night. Closed doors do not matter. All cheating, lying, trickery, backstabbing and stealing, I see.*"

I stood up after hearing all this. It got quiet, not a sound was made. I nearly needed to be picked up off the floor. All the time my mind was trying to process what I was seeing and hearing. Then God started to speak again: "My angels are there recording it all. No one can get away with being dishonest. No one can hide from me where I cannot find them or see and hear what they are doing with their lives. I am *God*!"

Psalm 138:6 (MSG)

**And here's why: GOD, high above, sees far below;
no matter the distance, he knows everything about us.**

As I stood there, I felt a sense of amazement. I thought about the times when I had stolen, lied, or cheated as a child or a teen. I felt shocked that he knew everything I had ever done—*everything*! God saw all the things *of* and *in* my life, wow just to think he saw all of it and I stood there yet I could not think of things I did and I did not feel guilty, judged or condemned as if I were a prisoner or convicted of a crime.

He began to shout. My natural mind could not understand his words, but somehow I felt like something was being imparted within me that allowed me to understand what he was saying.

Then to my amazement, I saw a drawer open up before me. There was a light that came on as it opened up that illuminated half of the drawer. Only the backside of the drawer was lit. I heard God's voice saying, *"This is your drawer."* What? I have my own drawer? Wow! Then God said, *"This one represents your life and what you have accomplished in your life up until now. The other part is dark; meaning you haven't lived or experienced it yet."*

My drawer, and all the other drawers, started to close after those words, and all their lights were going off. Then God spoke again to me, saying, *"Tell the people on the earth that their lives are an open book to me. They may think I do not exist, but I do. Tell them to just look around at all they see. It was all created by me, even the earth they live on. The day will come when all who have walked this earth will stand before me, just like you're standing here before me now son. All will give an account for their lives and their deeds done on earth."*

Philippians 1:28-29 (MSG)

Let nothing in your conduct hang on whether I come or not. Your conduct must be the same whether I show up to see things for myself or hear of it from a distance.

I realized I was not up there to give an account of my life. I was there to be shown that God has a divine order. God would speak, then be silent, and then speak again. That is how he expressed himself. This allowed me time to process

His words.

He spoke again and said, "*Listen son, you must tell them no one is excused from standing before me. It does not matter their name or rank. All presidents, kings and queens are accountable to me—even the beggar that you see standing on the street. All the people on the earth will give an account for their lives, from the richest person to the poorest. I never stop watching or recording.*"

I am reminded of a song called "God is watching" by Bette Midler. Now let me ask you this: Are you dishonest in the affairs of your life? Are you always trying to beat the system, cut corners, make false statements, or cheat on your books in business? If so, why—when doing right works so much better? In addition, when you do make the right choices, I don't know about but you, but I just feel good inside. I would like to say this, God put a standard in the earth to govern this world. How do I know? He gave us the law and officers to carry out His will and for them to protect us. The bible says they are the authority on earth. He calls them ministering spirits just for us. As I said before God is watching all of us.

Next, I was shown the monies that are in the world. God showed me the scales, balances and weights. His voice said, "*I know ounces, pounds and tons. I have seen it all.*" The Lord said, "*Men who think they can change the scales to rob—be forewarned. I see everything, and no one can get away with being crooked in business. They may fool the buyer, but the seller knows and so do I because every transaction done has been recorded. Business owners have a set of books and so do I. They will have to give an account of their dealing where money is concerned. Many have already been exposed publicly and by their own choosing brought destruction upon themselves. They have brought shame on their families and lost all they own.*"

God then instructed me to let men know that every dishonest gain is always being recorded—even that done on a small scale —for no one will ever get away with any wrongdoing.

As I stood there, this thought crossed my mind; some men must think that they can get away with anything. They think they can hide their actions from God, but He is watching us all the time. We are never alone. **When you think you are the only one in the room—smile! You are on God's camera** and the tape is rolling. You are the star of your own show. Isn't it remarkable how God uses the media to expose dishonest people all around the world? It is time for us to know that everything we do is being recorded, both good and bad. **Whether our net worth is one billion or one cent**, all of us will give an account of how we treated people on this earth.

Going to the records room in heaven was a real revelation for me. I hope that as you read this you will make the right choices. Since God is watching us, the worst thing we can do is try to cover up our lifestyles. Do you want the whole world to know about what you have done? The Bible says, "Your crooked ways will destroy you!"

Proverbs 11:3 The Message (MSG)

The integrity of the honest keeps them on track; the deviousness of crooks brings them to ruin.

Some may have lawyers and can pay the judges to cover up what they did. It does not matter—they are still going to face their Creator. Through knowledge of God's goodness, we can be honest, even in a dishonest world in which we live. There is a way of escape—by making the right choices and living right. Let it be *you* who makes a difference in this world.

I stood and stared at all those files. I kept thinking of deals done on earth behind closed doors. The price will be higher for all cons, cheaters and liars. Do not find yourself being one of them! It is better to be honest in your affairs in life than to be on the world news known as a common crook. The Bible has a lot to say about doing right.

Proverbs 12:12The Message (MSG)

What the wicked construct finally falls into ruin, while the roots of the righteous give life, and more life.

I knew I had to move on, but there was just something about the Records Room. I could feel God's heartbeat there. All the action on earth is dear to him; for our lives are very important. None of us is just a number.

While I was there, I also saw a building as if through a glass wall. It was open and I could see real-life scenes of everyday families living in each room. In one, I saw a man putting a needle in his arm. The expression on his face showed that he felt no hope; no other way to face life or reality. In another room, I saw a husband and wife arguing over finances. The husband was upset and walked out the door. I knew he was not coming back. One of the scenes was of a dark room with a little girl laying on a bed and an elderly adult climbing in the bed with her. She had a look of stark terror on her face. It made me sick in my stomach. Now I questioned God: *How could this happen?*

He said, "*What you're seeing is the evil on the earth. These are real-life situations.*" In one of the rooms I heard screaming and cursing and the slamming of doors. A teenage girl was screaming and cursing at her mother, "I hate you! I hate you! I hate you!" She was wishing she had never been born. In the final room, I saw a man sitting with a bottle of whiskey. What really caught my attention was the picture of his family that he was holding in his hand. He had seemingly decided to drink his life away. I could see the hurt, emptiness, and loneliness on his face. It seemed that his life was over, and there was not anything that was going to help his sadness. I just stood and stared at it all for what seemed like eternity.

Reading this may make you think about your family, and what they are going through that you do not know about we all need love love. However, I tell you that God knows. It has all been recorded in His Records Room. My friend, I challenge you to re-read this repeatedly. Grasp the real meaning of this room.

As I stood there, all the drawers and lights went off. It was time to go—and I was ready. I started to walk back down that hall. It seemed like an eternity back in time. As I walked, I noticed that the wood in the hall seemed to be stained with blood. My mind went back to Jesus on the cross. I remembered what God had said: "If only they would know Me and my way of doing things!" There was a different atmosphere going back. I had a feeling of freedom and pure excitement. I did not remember what I had done in the past. It was as if it had never happened. All was forgiven and forgotten and all had been washed away.

I felt joy, love, and peace—like a child at Christmas time. Imagine you are coming down the stairs on Christmas morning. You are by yourself, everyone else is asleep. You see all the presents and decorations, and then you focus on *your* package—the one with your name on it. In addition, you are overcome with excitement. This is my explanation of how I felt walking down that hall. It was very different.

To my surprise, there was my missing-in-action angel. I looked at him and thought, *why did he leave me?* Wondering, *why did I have to go down this hall alone?* Could it be that I was supposed to see myself and how I really am? Just maybe, God wanted me to change things in my life by showing me all of this.

When I came out of that hall the angel said, "*This next place has a lot to do with your ministry and what you are called to do on earth.*" I kept thinking about what the angel said concerning my purpose, my calling and why I am here on the earth.

You may have had the same thought at one time or another. You may have asked, *what is my purpose for being here?* I know why *I* am here, and it is to bring God's healing power to a sick and dying world. You may be wondering what I am talking about. Healing power flows through me. It comes from God; it is his gift to this world. As a doctor would use medicine to treat you or me, God uses people that have the gifts of healing to do his doctoring.

Then the angel said, *"You have a healing ministry!"* I said, *"That's right!"* The world has not been exposed to the kind of healing ministry that is coming. What seems to be impossible to man, I have witnessed God do. I know this and other healing ministries are going to be worldwide so get ready to see His power move like never before. He is going to manifest his power with undeniable and unexplainable healings. It will be God's doing, not man's. Nevertheless, he will work though man to accomplish his will in this world.

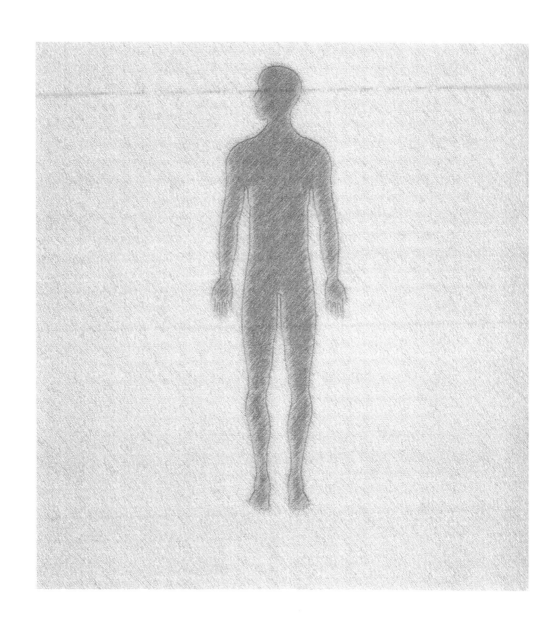

Did you know God has a parts room?

Now I have your attention don't I? The next place I visited floored me. When the angel began to speak, I looked at him squarely in the eyes. He looked back into mine with the same intensity. I grew still and waited for him to speak. Suddenly he lit up and said, *"We are going to another place now."*

If you do not believe in angels, you may think what I am about to describe is nonsense; you may even think I am nuts. However, the angel said, "We are going to the parts room." I said aloud, *"The parts room!"* I thought, *what does this room have to do with me?*

Next, we came to an entrance without doors. I thought, *how do we get into this place?* The angel took my arm and said, *"Are you ready for this?"* We then walked right through a glass wall. As we did, I felt a wind blow right through me, just like the one I had felt while being transported into heaven! I kept looking around. This place was big—and unbelievable. A silvery-blue mist floated above the floor. The *parts room* was huge. This room looked to have about fifty massive bookshelves made out of glass in it, rows and rows of them with about fifty shelves in each row.

The angel put his hand on my shoulder and said, *"Get closer,"* which I did. What I saw so astonished me my mind could not comprehend it. A force grabbed me and drew me in like a vacuum!

I said aloud, *"Body parts! Body parts for God's creation!"* I nearly exploded. It was awesome to say the least. I saw eyes and organs, there was a heart, a pair of lungs, and even what appeared to be a brain. There were limbs;

legs and arms.

The angel replied, "*Yes, that's right*! You see everything needed on earth for all mankind is right here." My mind went wild with excitement, and I felt real joy. Then the angel said, "*It's all here, and God did not leave anything out.*" According to heaven, all we have to do is believe it! People should not say they believe if they really do not because God knows whether they do or not. The angel then praised God and said, "*God is the only creator of all living things.*"

You need to know this for sure; whatever you need, God has it. If you can get real and believe in God, then everything, and I mean *everything* you need—God has it! You must believe in him as the Creator of all things. Anyone can believe in him and anyone can know him. I know in my heart that I came from him. If you were to go to a pond of fish and frogs and the fish could miraculously talk, they would say the same thing I am saying. They would bubble up out of the water and say, "Get real people. God created us too!"

Genesis 1:26 (MSG)

God spoke: "Let us make human beings in our image, make them reflecting our nature.

Reading about the parts room, you might think I am nuts. One day however, we will all see for ourselves that heaven is a real place and not some made-up fairyland. One day everyone on earth will know that angels are real and that anything that we believe in God to do, he can and will do! You see, God took me to heaven, and he has allowed me to remember my trip there so I could tell you about my experience.

Now I want to ask you something. When your car or truck breaks down, what do you do? You probably take it to a mechanic or garage where it can be repaired. When your body gets hurt or you feel sick, you probably go and see a doctor or check into a hospital. Whichever part of your body is not working, you probably expect the doctor to find out what the cause is and take care of it.

Now, keep all this in mind and let me share with you about men and women who have healing ministries. They are like God's doctors on the earth. God is not there physically, but he is there in the Spirit. When people use gifts of healing for God, it produces the natural effect of healing. He is there even though you cannot see him. Something happens. Some people may feel cold or hot before they are healed. Some feel a warm flow throughout their body. Others may feel a breeze flowing through them. I have even had people say to me that they felt an electrical shock. They realize that something has changed, and they can do things they could not do before. They jump for joy, very relieved, thanking the Lord for their miracle.

To them, it is a miracle to have a dead leg begin to work, or a bad back begin to straighten up. Many will go back to the doctor who then confirms it. Often the doctor cannot explain it. Even some doctors call it a miracle! I myself have laid hands on people, and they were healed. You see, I am just an instrument of God's healing power. His healing power and gifts flow through me to others.

I Peter 2:9 (MSG)

But you are the ones chosen by God, chosen for the high calling of priestly work, chosen to be a holy people, God's instruments to do his work and speak out for him, to tell others of the night-and-day difference he made for you—from nothing to something, from rejected to accepted.

Let me explain what happens to me. I sometimes feel a sensation that comes over me, I may feel heat in my left hand. Sometimes it feels as though it is stuck in a vice. It feels as though I have a hand-warmer in my hand, or like putting your hands toward a hot fire. Whenever this feeling comes on, I know the anointing is there to heal them. Though I cannot see God there physically, I know he is there in the Spirit. A miracle is about to happen, as the evidence of His presence.

Acts 2:4 (MSG)

When the Feast of Pentecost came, they were all together in one place. Without warning there was a sound like a strong wind, gale force—no one could tell where it came from. It filled the whole building. Then, like a wildfire, the Holy Spirit spread through their ranks, and they started speaking in a number of different languages as the Spirit prompted them.

God heals and He should get all the credit. You could have a condition that you are seeing a doctor about. Therefore, with that in mind I ask God to heal YOU right now! I ask that his healing power grab a hold of you while you are reading this. May he surround you with his love and heal you of every sickness right now! I believe God will do it for anyone.

I know I am an instrument that He uses. He simply restores or removes whatever is needed in people. He made you and he knows you, even if you do not know him. When God heals, it is like this: Once blind, now you can see. Once deaf, now you can hear. Once in a wheelchair, now you can walk. Once dead, now you are alive! I have seen many miracles and every time I see one, I am still amazed. I could go on and on talking about healing. I could write another book about the many signs and wonders that I have seen. Now that is an idea!

When I was seventeen years old, I gave my heart and life to the Lord. I am putting down on paper what I have experienced. This may be hard for you to believe but many miracles, signs, and wonders are still happening.

Mark 3:1-3 (MSG)

Then he went back in the meeting place where he found a man with a crippled hand. The Pharisees had their eyes on Jesus to see if he would heal him, hoping to catch him in a Sabbath infraction. He said to the man with the crippled hand, "Stand here where we can see you."

Heaven is real! When you have seen the things I have, or even a small part, you will never be the same. I never doubted God's healing power or his power to do the impossible. Learning his word put his power into action in my life so that others can receive their healing. Miracles can happen every day for people if they believe. He is the great doctor of all doctors. The same can happen for you if you learn his word and incorporate it into your life as well. I see myself as his intern, and I am always learning from him. Sometimes I skipped classes, but God still used me and taught me. It takes years of studying and hands on training to be a doctor. I have found God uses the same method for spiritual training. When you are his pupil, he trains you and teaches you his word so that you can use it to pray for others to be healed by his Spirit. In time, he will release you to be his doctor on the earth—but He gets all the credit.

This chapter has probably floored you. Your mind is probably having all kinds of images floating through it. Like me, you may have all kinds of questions regarding who, what, where, when, why and how. That is understandable, and what I have described does seem unbelievable.

Our natural minds see and hear things. Sometimes the things we see and hear can set us back. We try so hard to figure it out, but we cannot. We ask, how can these things be? It is during these times we can turn to God to show us what is going on and how to process these things and move forward.

Now moving on to our next place in heaven--

I am sure you have heard the song, "Follow the yellow brick road?" Ring a bell? Sure it does. Why, that is the song in the movie we all love to see called *The Wizard of Oz*. Remember those days when we were growing up, some of us could not wait to see it. Now that I have your attention, the angel said, "*All we have to do to is to follow the streets of gold. Yes, I said gold.*"

As we walked down these streets of gold, we could see right through them. They were simply breathtaking. I could see everything in fine detail, all the buildings, big and small. It was as if God had taken a special tool and etched out unique designs in everything, each with its own unique style. **All the elements fit together**, yet each stood out by itself. Everything displayed God's designer ways and his artistic ability. Amazing colors were displayed everywhere I looked.

Our master designer must delight in bringing pleasure to operate by allowing man to catch a glimpse of heaven. There are others who have gone there, for I have heard many stories—including other accounts of *out of body* experiences. It was phenomenal for me to be able to go there and to come back and share what I saw, felt, and knew while I was there. I mentioned earlier the bouquets of flowers everywhere. Each flower had its own smell, and when I stood in front of them, I could smell the whole bouquet. In heaven, there were grassy fields, gorgeous waterfalls and trees of every size, shape, and color. Some may be wondering about the temperature in heaven. It was perfect—not too hot or too cold. It was just right, as if it were tailor made for me. As I kept walking, I noticed something bright in the distance. It seemed to be moving, so I drew closer. It was glistening! What a sight! I nearly fainted when I saw it up close, for it was a sea. That is right—there was a sea in heaven. It was a glass sea moving back and forth and shining brightly.

Then the angel stepped up and said, "*We need to move on; time is running out.*" I said to him, "*I don't want to go back! I want to stay here. Are you sure, I can't stay? Can we make a deal?*" He said, "*No, you have to go back and tell the people on earth about heaven.*" I found myself arguing with the angel of the Lord. Could I be in trouble now? The angel replied, "*They have to be told, and they all need to know what God has in store for them.*" Then he said, "*God has commanded you to go back and tell them how to come here.*" I knew that I would be going back and that this was just a visit. It was not yet my time to come and live here forever.

EXPERIENCE 6 - SOUNDS OF HEAVEN

If you love music, then you are going to love this. There is a music room in heaven. The best way I can describe it is as a large orchestra playing—but without players. The instruments—of all shapes, sizes, and sounds were playing themselves. The music room was filled with heavenly sounds of praise music. I was beside myself and taken aback. I got closer, and I could distinguish the sound—trumpets and horns of all kinds. One that especially caught my ear was a French horn. It was the most wonderful sound that one could ever hear. I have never heard a sound on earth like it.

I was caught up in the sounds coming from heaven's musical room, Heaven is where I want to be!

I felt whole in heaven; I had pure joy, and no pain. In the Bible's creation account, Heaven was first and then the earth was second. Based on what I experienced, earth is a carbon copy of heaven. Only heaven is better than earth! There is no sickness, disease, pain, or death in heaven—only life, joy, and peace!

Do you remember the presence and energy I described feeling during this experience? It stayed with me the entire time I was in heaven, but now it became even stronger. It was like pure energy, and I never ever felt tired or sleepy—only refreshed, all the time.

As I walked, I saw people who looked familiar. I recognized one man for sure. I would read about him in the Bible, in the Old Testament. He was a prophet who did amazing things for God. It was Jeremiah! He looked just as you might imagine an Old Testament prophet would. *Wow*, I thought, *I know everybody here.*

I heard laughing around me. I turned and saw children of all ages playing and laughing. I thought for a minute, *where did all these children come from.* I then remembered the aborted babies on earth. These were the many children whose lives had been taken away from them. They had to grow up somewhere, and they had come from the earth to complete their lives in heaven and live forever. There were both girls and boys, having a good time, running around with joy and contentment on their faces. They looked at me as if I were not a stranger, but one of them—like family. There was so much to see; everything was so pleasant to my eyes.

There is still much to tell, and I know there are things that I don't remember. All I can leave you with is this; heaven is a wonderful, eternal place, and I cannot wait to go back. My heart's desire was to bring back this experience in such a way that all can understand it. God wants us to know that heaven is real, and he designed it for his creation. It is for every single soul on earth, but they must believe in God like never before. If heaven were a secret, then why would God let us know about it? The fact that so many have experienced heaven just shows that God wants us to know about it. While we are alive on this earth, many of us can enjoy our lives more knowing that there is a heaven and knowing that there is life after death. The possibility of going to heaven is something wonderful for us all to look forward to.

Now, here I go again down the streets of gold!

The angel pulled on my arm and said, "*We have to move on.*" Even though there are times and schedules on earth, this is not true in heaven. I noticed the angel wasn't wearing a watch, but my time there was scheduled. From there, we walked a little farther and something else caught my eye. I saw a figure standing. It was Jesus himself! Just as I walked by, he turned, looked at me, and smiled. I did not say a word to him, and he did not speak to me. We just looked at each other.

The next thing I knew, I was walking again. I felt as if I was leaving. I walked along these gold streets thinking, *what a place*! Then, I wondered, *Could I get this message across to the people on the earth? How will I tell them? How do I start?*

Then the angel came and put his hand on my shoulder, and all my thoughts were calm. I was at rest. Looking ahead, something again caught my attention. I saw big, bright white objects that looked like unique shells. I could see them clearly. As I got closer, I knew that these were gates made out of pearls. They looked as if someone had used a sharp knife or tool to design them. They were simply beautiful. I noticed that they were closed, but there was not any lock on them. The Bible refers to gates made of pearls in

Revelation 21:21 (MSG)

"The twelve gates were twelve pearls, each gate a single pearl."

Were these the gates that passage refers to? I really don't know. I was seeing all this for the first time. Could there be more? I will let you decide for yourself.

I knew I was almost at the end of this experience. You may wonder how I knew. All I can say is that in heaven you know things beforehand. You recognize people up there, and you know what you are looking at even if your eyes have never seen it before. Some of your thoughts, (not all), are answered when you think them, and that is what amazed me. All my questions were being answered right away in my mind. I know all of this may be a bit much to take in. That's ok, I am not the only one who has gone to heaven and come back to talk about it.

As we consider the next place—called the ***throne room***—you may be in deep thought over everything you have read already. This room, even though it is the last room, was the largest I saw, and the most active. There were all kinds of heavenly beings and people within it. You may have heard stories or seen plays about a throne room. There have been movies about heaven that portrayed God sitting on his heavenly throne. Sometimes he is giving out orders on earth. I have wondered, *how many directors read the Bible before they make their movies?*

I will say this; I did not witness God sitting in heaven giving orders to people. He is not up there ready to pounce on us, saying, "If you don't obey me, then I will zap you off the earth!" That's Hollywood's version not God's. God is not a monster. He is a loving Father. Why does Hollywood suggest that we can live and act any way we want and still go to heaven? It is simple: They do not know him—or the truth!

Now, ladies and gentlemen can I have a drum roll ... **I was taken into the throne room**! When the angel took me in, it outdid all of my previous experiences in heaven. Oh, the wonders my eyes saw! It is the most beautiful place in all of heaven. This place astounded me. As the angel took me into the throne room he said, *"Notice, you are standing on a square on the floor". Do you see these squares, and these people standing here? This is their meeting place. Some squares are full and some are empty. No one can take your place up here, and all these squares are assigned to certain people."*

Revelation 7:9 (MSG)

I looked again. I saw a huge crowd, too huge to count. Everyone was there—all nations and tribes, all races and languages. And they were *standing*, dressed in white robes and waving palm branches, standing before the Throne and the Lamb and heartily singing:

Then there was complete silence. Even the angel that I was with transformed into a lower being. It was as if he was transcended into another realm, where there was evidence of a greater power in our presence. He stopped communicating with me. He did not move, and I stood and watched while he was changed and subdued by this power. It was as if he was receiving instructions, and I was not even there. I did not move or say anything, I froze! All I could do was watch, listen, and take it all in.

The throne room looked like a command center for the whole world. It reminded me of a large TV studio where a great production was getting ready to be produced with a lot of activity as I was watching. As I was looking at the floor, I noticed that clouds were moving around my feet, up to my knees. There was also a mist or smoke. I was so overwhelmed with the feeling I was experiencing. It is hard to describe, but it was very moving.

So there I was, standing in the throne room. There were flashes of lightning all around me and sounds of thunder echoing around the room. A strong voice rose up and spoke with authority. It could be heard everywhere, and angels were visible everywhere.

I know that people have a certain image of angels in their minds. They may picture babies with wings floating through the air playing harps, or Cupid with a bow and arrow. If those are the angels that are to take care of us when we are in trouble, then I would say no thank you. Some artists portray them nude, with long, flowing, feathery wings. In addition, some are portrayed as women. I am sorry to tell you I did not see that in heaven. The ones I saw were male angels, and they were very strong and tall, with power and authority. They also had long blonde hair, and their skin was a bronze color. They would stand and have the presence that whatever is standing in front of them is going to move out of their way, no questions asked. God said he gives his angels charge over us. Do you want a baby with wings that can't save themselves watching over you?

I heard a noise that caught my attention, and all the angels started to bow down. I heard a sound like a roar from the throne. Then the angel said to me, "*It is time to bow*," and he pushed me to the floor with his hand on my back. Everybody hit the floor and bowed down. There I was on the floor wondering what was going to happen next. *Will we hear a voice again? What will I see? If I do hear a voice, what will it say, and will I understand it?* All kinds of questions went through my mind–with the answers, as usual, coming to me as well. Sometimes my mind would just run away from me but then something would come over me and I would become calm again; like a real peace that's the only way I can say it.

As I bowed on the floor, I noticed that it was a shining blue and white color. It seemed to have two shades of blue in it. There were clouds moving about and there was a mist. Was it clouds or was it mist? I do not know. It was simply floating over the floor as I bowed down. It looked as if the floor was moving and standing still at the same time. I raised my head up to see what was going on. I had to know! I saw some angels parting their wings standing in the front around the throne. There were different types of angels. Some had four sets of wings and some just two. The wings seemed to be seven or eight feet tall. As their wings parted, bright white lights appeared and grew even brighter. There was also a blue cast coming through their parted wings. The angels with four sets of wings had two on top above their shoulder blades and two on the middle of their backs.

These angels around the throne were different from the ones I had already seen. I could hear thunder as they parted their wings. A bright light covered them all each time they parted and opened their wings. I felt another surge of pure energy.

Then I heard another noise. Suddenly, what I would call, the elite messengers of God would take off from each side of the throne. When one group took off, another group would return and take the place where the previous group stood. When I saw them come in, they looked as if they had just come back from war. There was an aura covering these angels. Still, the mist allowed me to see them only partially. They had a covering on them when they came in, and I noticed that their countenances had changed. There was a difference about the way they looked and acted. It seemed that the bright light energized them and brought them back whole to their original state. They did not look like they were battered from war anymore. (Why I call it a war I do not know. It was simply apparent that they had come back from some sort of confrontation.)

The next thing I saw stunned me to the bone. I heard another noise—a voice. As I looked up, I could not make out what I was seeing, but then it became clear. Picture the Lincoln Memorial. That is what it reminded me of—that big chair with President Abraham Lincoln sitting on it. In a similar way, I saw a big chair, and on it sat a shadow or an image of a man. I, however, could not see a real man, I could only say it appeared to be an image of a man. Lighting was shooting out from this chair. I heard crashing sounds and saw big flashes of light.

Then I heard an amazing voice and I looked up. In front of me was the image of a man of fire walking around that throne. It was not a man *on* fire, but a man *made of* fire. If I had to guess who that was, I would say the Holy Spirit. Then I heard a loud roar. The man of fire disappeared and I did not see him anymore. I wondered where he went. Meanwhile, the angels were coming in and out. I do not know how to put into words what I felt, but there was a powerful force in that room. Angels were all around the throne.

Revelation 5:7 (MSG)

I looked again. I heard a company of Angels around the Throne, the Animals, and the Elders—ten thousand times ten thousand their number, thousand after thousand after thousand in full song:

Then I saw an altar, and on this altar were fiery stones about as big as a man's hand. First, there was a sound coming from the throne. An angel came repeatedly to the altar, picked up a fiery stone, and left with it. This was going on the entire time I was there. Sometimes the angels would pick up more than one stone at a time.

I had a similar experience here on earth in a meeting I was leading in Dallas, Texas in 1989. I was praying for people in a healing line. I heard a voice say to me, "Reach up here and get a stone off the altar." I acted out what I saw and heard. I felt intense heat in my hand as I held it and was instructed to put it on top of the woman's head.

When I did so, she described an explosion she felt happening in her stomach. She fell to the floor and received her healing. She had had cancer in her body. She came the next night with a doctor's report in her hand stating that she had no cancer. The doctor noted a miracle on the bottom of the report. She was excited and thanked the Lord for giving her such a miracle.

I had nothing to do with it. It was God and God alone. Isn't that amazing that the altar in the throne room coincides with the things on the earth? There is an event recorded in the Old Testament in which a prophet called down fire from heaven.

II Kings 1:10 (MSG)

Elijah answered the captain of the fifty, "If it's true that I'm a 'holy man,' lightning strike you and your fifty men!" Out of the blue lightning struck and incinerated the captain and his fifty.

Jesus spoke very plainly about the Holy Spirit coming, and when it happened, it was described as "cloven tongues like as of fire" You can find the whole story in the New Testament, in the Book of Acts chapter 2. Flames appeared on top of the disciples' heads.

Most of us wonder at times what heaven must *really* be like. I know how you feel. I was just that way until my experience of being there. Heaven to me has become a reality—a living, breathing reality. I hope you can see in your mind what I saw, as you have read my story about heaven. It was so breath taking beautiful!

You may be wondering, *was that Jesus sitting on that throne?* I know Jesus is God's right-hand man, and they work together. Father and Son Company, that is right! As I was looking toward the throne, I saw the world, and a cross. I saw Jesus on that cross, and his blood was flowing out of his body, running onto the earth. It reminded me of

John 3:16: (MSG)

"This is how much God loved the world: He gave his Son, his one and only Son. And this is why: so that no one need be destroyed; by believing in him, anyone can have a whole and lasting life. God didn't go to all the trouble of sending his Son merely to point an accusing finger, telling the world how bad it was. He came to help, to put the world right again. Anyone who trusts in him is acquitted; anyone who refuses to trust him has long since been under the death sentence without knowing it. And why? Because of that person's failure to believe in the one-of-a-kind Son of God when introduced to him.

In the center of that throne, I saw the earth. I saw the image of the cross-wedged within the earth. Jesus was hanging on the cross over the world. As I was still kneeling, looking up at this sight, it became a living reality; something I will never forget.

This experience in heaven is living eternally within me. There I was, taking it all in, and I could hear heaven's orchestra playing. Some might presume it was praise music that was playing. It was ringing out from everywhere. There was a wind blowing releasing peace and comfort. It was swirling all around me while I was still bowed down. When the angels closed their wings, I was standing up and the angel was telling me, "*You're getting ready to go back!*" I did not say a word but noticed, that all my questions were still being answered as I thought them. I was thinking, *I have to remember everything I am seeing, hearing, and feeling*.

As I thought that, I heard the words, "*I want you to write a book about heaven and all you have experienced.*" He also said, "*I'll let you know when to release the book.*" It has been a few years, but I still remember this as if it were yesterday. That is why I live so free; I know what awaits me. There is life after death, so why should I ever be afraid? Sure, people will miss me when I die. However, when I die I will live again—with God in heaven.

I will never forget the sights, the sounds, the feelings, and the experience of being in this place called heaven. There is no one on earth who can convince me I did not experience this, or that I did not go to heaven because it will be forever imprinted on my mind. This is something utterly real for me, and I will never again worry about my life down here. I will just listen to the voice of God, and love people as he does. In addition, I will let you be the judge.

When I die, I will exit this life to a new life in heaven, which is beyond comprehension. It is joyful living and fearless living. You can judge my words, but you can never take away my experience in heaven—ever!

While bowing in the throne room I sensed that this was a command center for the whole world. No one told me so, but I had a sense that this is what it was. There was a lot of activity going on, like a TV studio where things are being readied for production. I was given the honor of visiting this great place.

This fact was driven home to me; God is in control of everything. He made you, all living things, and me. Everything came from him! He made all that we enjoy on this earth. Some would call it *Mother Nature*, but in reality, it's *Father God*! I have seen the place where his will is being done and his commands are carried out by his angels.

Another point about my experience while walking to the throne room; I saw a wall. Picture a bricklayer who makes a wall of concrete. While it is still wet, he picks up stones of different colors, and some crushed diamonds, and throws them into the wall. That is what I am trying to describe here. There were many colored stones and diamonds, that were crushed and were all mixed and set in the wall. It was just beautiful.

If you could see that wall, the streets, the sights, and all that heaven has, you would literally be speechless. You would see the God who made you. This God has something great planned for all of us. We just need to believe in Him. You have to have faith.

This account is almost at an end, even though there is more to see along the solid gold streets. This thought came to me as I was walking around in heaven, I have heard that God is a mystery and you cannot really know and understand him, when the opposite is true. You have to stop right here and ask yourself if he didn't want us to know him, then why has he been involved in our affairs since the beginning of time. It is really a simple answer; He cares about us.

I walked back on the path I remembered from before when I first came and met the angel. I knew it was time to go back to earth, and my visit was ending. As I walked to the entrance with the angel, I noticed that I was transferred into the same tunnel as before, with lights and clouds. I went down the same way I had gone up.

There I was, traveling down the same tunnel. As before, I was moving slowly at first, and then picked up speed. I went faster and faster. I came out of the tunnel and there I was flying in midair above the city of Dallas, over my home. I saw the cars and buildings, still small and very far away. I noticed how light I felt floating through the air. As I got closer, I felt as if the very same suit that had come off me before was now back on. I fell right into it. It was heavy. Now I was returning to earth; I was no longer light and free. A force was pulling me down. I could not see it, but I could definitely feel it.

One day, I hope to find out the answer about that suit that was put back on me and what it was all about when I came back into this earth. *What was that thing?*

Now I was coming in for a landing, getting closer to earth. Wow, sounds like I was on an airplane. Well let me say that I was not on a plane I was my own airplane. If you are wondering if I had my arms out like a plane, no I did not. I was just flying in the air, there was no angel holding me and I did not have any wings on the back of my body.

Soon I began hearing the sounds of the city returning to me. The cars running and horns blowing; airplanes coming in and going out. I could see people walking. I went by a traffic light; it was red. At first glance, I thought I was going to run right in to it, but I flew right under it.

Come to think of it that is the way heaven's beings or the angels I saw got around the world. I have often wondered how they do it, what is their fuel? My first guess is angel food cake, just joking, but in reality it has to do with God and his power. *Wow, this is the way to travel—just take off, and land.*

There is one other thing I would like to say; I never once thought about food. That is very unusual for me because when I go to a new place, I'm always wanting to know if there is any food there to eat. You can ask anybody that knows me.

The next thing I knew I was going right down through the roof and then the ceiling of my condominium down, down, down. I saw my body, once again, lying on the floor. It looked as if I was in a deep sleep I almost looked dead. I saw Samson laid out, not moving at all. He looked dead! I went into my body as easily as I had gone out. Nothing to it, it did not hurt at all. There was still no fear or pain only peace.

This was just amazing, how could you go and come back into something and not feel a thing. I have to stop here and say-- is Heaven really just a breath away? I leave it to you to come up with the answer for that one.

As I woke up, my body began to move around. I looked at my cat. He did not move, so I started moving his legs, paws, ears, and tail. He did not have much life in him. I told God, *"You killed my cat; he's not moving. What did I do?"* I was pulling on Samson, and then he woke up and shook his head. He stuck out his tongue, and even tried to bite me. I pushed him away and said, *"You haven't changed a bit!"* He looked at me, stood up, stretched out his limp body, and left the room. I was thinking about what Samson might have experienced while he was out. I think he just got a real good sleep.

As I lay on the floor thinking about what just happened to me. How would I be able to explain it all? I was puzzled, but I knew it *had* happened. I knew God had taken me to heaven. I had so many questions. I talked to myself and tried to reason with myself. I even went to the bathroom and threw water on my face, thinking, *am I going crazy? Have I snapped?* Then I said, *"I would sit down and write what I saw as I remember it. I want to make it simple so that everyone who reads this book will understand what I am saying.*

As readers think about the unknown, they may find themselves wondering, *Is there really life after death?* And *Is there another real place like the one this person is talking about that he experienced? Here I am reading about what he saw and experienced, yet my own mind puts up mental blocks.*

I would like to say for all the millions of people out there wondering the same thing; that's why God is always saying we see with our heart and not our head. It has always been this way. I have trained myself to believe this; to ask God to let me see how He sees. Your mind fights what you see.

If that describes you, I can truthfully say, I know how you feel. Even as I was standing in heaven seeing the things that I saw, my mind had the same difficulties understanding that you may be having. You will have to get the answers you seek from God. Our natural mind cannot comprehend everything about God.

It does not matter where you are in this life, you can come to the reality of heaven. Some of the questions you may have had about heaven may have been answered after reading this book.

I cannot tell you I know all of it. I encourage you to seek out this God and heaven that I am telling you about. Seek to have your own experience and not just take my word for it based on my experience. I know the bible says only God himself can show you and I the truth. He can explain to us the truth about what he has in store for us.

Heaven is something he has in store for his creation, and that means life after death. Moreover, I can truly say this for a fact, God is all about living, not dying!

I know there are a great deal of people that are probably in shock over what you just read about heaven. The next question most likely running through your mind is, *Is God so personable that I can really know him*? Yes you can, we are talking about God. The one that created you and me and heaven and earth. The one who took me to heaven and showed me his big house that he lives in; that's the one.

FOOD FOR THOUGHT

Let me break this down. Do you have a friend that you talk to? Why sure, we all do. In my many experiences I often talk to God. You might be saying to yourself, now wait a minute. I cannot see him, so how can I even talk with him?

Checkmate! Let's think about this. If I were to call you on the phone and you answer, and I said how are you doing Fred? I'm over here in another state just thinking about you and your family. Now here is the kicker, you really don't know what state I'm calling you from now do you? I could be in another country and you have no way of telling where I am. The only true way of knowing if I said to you where I was, is because you know that I am a man of my word.

Let me tell you God is real and wants to talk to us but he doesn't have a phone up in heaven like we have down here on earth. So how would he reveal himself to us? Let me put it this way; how would God talk directly to you?

This is the way we are designed. We have a body made of flesh but we also have a spirit. Now do you remember earlier when I would say if I had a thought it was answered without one word being said? Well that is your built in phone called your SPIRIT.

This is the way God will talk with you and you will know it and understand it. I have come to know His voice at an early age by Him talking to my spirit. God told me that he would also talk to me through His word, the bible.

Here comes the wall of doubt. What if I don't believe the bible? Then my friend, you just cut off your phone to him. I like to see the bible in this way; as a book of texts messages to me that I have not opened and read yet if you would start to only open up the texts messages that have to do with God first you would then start to learn and know more about him and what he is really like this is just a simple truth that i found out to be really true today for everyone that wants to text him.

Now to end this great and wonderful experience. When you are talking about God and heaven, there is no ending to the experience you could have with him. He wants **you** to know all there is to know about Him so you can find out about yourself. When you say to him GOD; how, when, where and why, He says you got a minute? Oh, wait what is that I hear? Your PHONE is ringing! I think its time for **YOU** to be TRANSCENDED!!

Tell Them

Tell them I am more than a friend,
Tell them I'll be there from now to the end.

Tell them I'm hope when there is none;
Tell them I'm waiting when they're on the run.

Tell them I've seen the good and the bad;
Tell them forgiveness is theirs to be had.

Tell them I've paid the ultimate price;
Tell them they're worthy of My sacrifice.

Tell them there's nothing they can do or say;
There's nothing they've done that will keep Me away.

Tell them My love will never run out;
Tell them there's nothing I don't know about.

Tell them that I have a plan for their life;
Tell them without Me there's nothing but strife.

Tell them that peace is waiting inside;
Tell them there's simply no place they can hide.

Tell them my name is I Am that I Am;
Tell them it's time that they take a stand.

Tell them by grace that I'll set them free;
Tell them they just need to come follow Me.

Dale Schrieber - 2014